12 POLITICAL LEADERS
WHO CHANGED THE WORLD

by Matthew McCabe

12 STORY LIBRARY

www.12StoryLibrary.com

12-Story Library is an imprint of Peterson Publishing Company and Press Room Editions.

Produced for 12-Story Library by Red Line Editorial

Photographs ©: Jerome Delay/AP Images, cover, 1, 22; Jacques Reich/Lea Brothers & Company/Library of Congress, 4; Peter Hermes Furian/iStockphoto, 5; Bain News Service/Library of Congress, 6; Library of Congress, 7; Bettmann/Corbis Images, 8, 17; Keren Su/Corbis Images, 9; J. Russell & Sons/Library of Congress, 10; Alfred/SIPA/AP Images, 12; Chris Hepburn/iStockphoto, 13, 28; F. Zucchero/Library of Congress, 14; Hulton Archive/iStockphoto, 15, 16; Flip Schulke/Corbis Images/© 1963 Dr. Martin Luther King, Jr. © renewed 1991 Coretta Scott King, 18; Warren K. Leffler/Library of Congress, 19, 29; Anthony Berger/Library of Congress, 20; Alexander Gardner/Library of Congress, 21; Carol M. Highsmith/Library of Congress, 23; Elias Goldensky/Library of Congress, 24; Carl Mydans/Farm Security Administration - Office of War Information Photograph Collection/Library of Congress, 25; Gilbert Stuart/Detroit Publishing Co./Library of Congress, 26; Percy Moran/Library of Congress, 27

ISBN
978-1-63235-148-7 (hardcover)
978-1-63235-189-0 (paperback)
978-1-62143-241-8 (hosted ebook)

Library of Congress Control Number: 2015934292

Printed in the United States of America
Mankato, MN
June, 2015

Go beyond the book. Get free, up-to-date content on this topic at 12StoryLibrary.com.

TABLE OF CONTENTS

ALEXANDER THE GREAT EXPANDS WORLD VIEWS

Alexander the Great was the world's first global leader. He led the Kingdom of Macedonia in 336 BCE. The kingdom was part of ancient Greece. Alexander achieved great military victories. He spread Greek culture to other parts of the world. At the time, the known world was much smaller than it is today. People rarely traveled outside their own town or kingdom.

Alexander was a talented military leader. He thought up new ways to defeat stronger forces. He organized his troops into groups called phalanxes. Soldiers stood shoulder to shoulder in several long rows. This prevented enemies

from successfully attacking them. Alexander also used cavalry to fight larger forces. Alexander led his army against the massive Persian Empire.

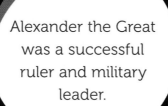

Alexander the Great was a successful ruler and military leader.

He defeated the Persians without losing a battle.

Alexander and his army traveled after beating the Persians. They covered more than 11,000 miles (17,703 km) in eight years. With the help of his army, Alexander founded 70 cities. His growing empire crossed Europe, Asia, and Africa. He opened trade routes between India and Europe. They were the first in human history. Greek language and culture united his empire. But Alexander also adopted foreign customs and languages. This helped him rule over the people he conquered.

2 million

Area, in square miles (5.18 million sq km), Alexander's empire covered.

- He spread Greek language and culture around the world.
- Alexander opened up the first trade routes between different regions of the world.
- He embraced foreign customs to help him rule.

Alexander the Great's empire covered three continents.

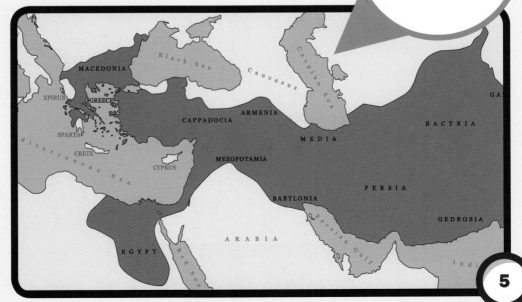

SUSAN B. ANTHONY LEADS US WOMEN FORWARD

Before 1920, only white men could vote in the United States. But many nineteenth-century women worked to change that. One of the most notable was Susan B. Anthony. She was born into a political family in 1820. She fought for a greater voice for women in American society.

During her childhood, Anthony's family fought to end slavery. She grew up listening to anti-slavery speeches. She attended anti-slavery meetings. She became passionate about the cause. In the 1850s, she organized anti-slavery meetings and speeches of her own. But her greatest effort was working to earn women the right to vote.

In Anthony's lifetime, women could not vote in the United States. Men controlled politics. They pursued policies that benefited them most. Women's political opinions were not taken seriously. In the 1870s, Anthony fought for women's suffrage, or right to vote. She traveled in the West to gather support. Her biggest move came in 1872. She voted for president. But this was against the

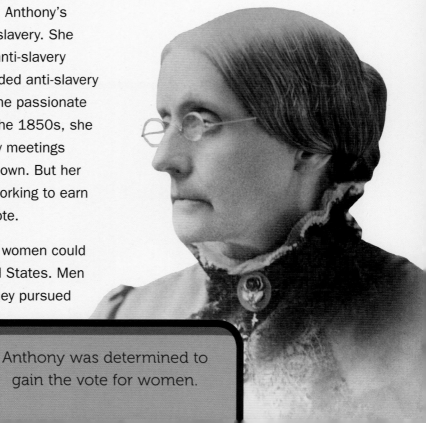

Anthony was determined to gain the vote for women.

Women demand the vote in Yonkers, New York, in 1913.

law. Anthony was arrested and fined $100. But she never paid the fine.

In 1877, Anthony helped found the National American Woman Suffrage Association. She led the suffrage movement until her death in 1906.

Women gained the right to vote in 1920. That is when the Nineteenth Amendment was passed. Some people called the law the Susan B. Anthony Amendment.

14

Years between Anthony's death and passage of the Nineteenth Amendment.

- Anthony fought for women's right to vote in the United States.
- She led suffrage associations and toured the country to gather support.
- She fought for equal pay for women.

ANTHONY'S OTHER CAUSES

Anthony's efforts gave women a voice in America. But she fought for many causes during her lifetime. She worked to get equal pay for female teachers. She supported women working in the printing trade. At the time, only men held these kinds of jobs. Anthony also wanted to give women the right to own property.

SIRIMAVO BANDARANAIKE LEADS SRI LANKA

Sirimavo Bandaranaike was elected prime minister of Sri Lanka in 1960. Her election changed the world. No woman had ever held a country's highest elected office. Bandaranaike helped create a national identity in Sri Lanka.

In 1948, Sri Lanka gained its independence from the United Kingdom. Bandaranaike's husband was its prime minister. He died in 1959. Bandaranaike took control of his political party. She won the election for prime minister a year later.

As prime minister, Bandaranaike made a lot of changes. She brought many industries under government

Bandaranaike at work after winning the election for prime minister in 1960

Bandaranaike made changes so more children could get an education.

control. Sri Lanka got rid of English as an official language. Educational opportunities were expanded. Native culture and heritage became school subjects. However, some people believe these changes came at a cost. Bandaranaike's efforts divided people in Sri Lanka. The majority Sinhalese people often benefited more from her policies. Minority Tamils often suffered.

Bandaranaike made many changes to Sri Lanka during her time in office. She stood up for Sri Lanka in discussions with other world leaders. These leaders were mostly men. There may be disagreement about her legacy. But Bandaranaike showed the world a woman could run a country.

18

Number of years Bandaranaike served as prime minister of Sri Lanka.

- Bandaranaike provided strong leadership in the years after Sri Lanka's independence.
- She expanded educational opportunities to more Sri Lankans.
- She showed the world women could lead a modern country.

THINK ABOUT IT

Often, world leaders make decisions people disagree with. Think of a rule or law you disagree with. Write a paragraph explaining why you disagree. Use examples to back up your opinion.

WINSTON CHURCHILL STANDS ALONE

Winston Churchill was the prime minister of the United Kingdom. He led the country during World War II (1939–1945). In the early years of the war, his country faced Germany alone. France had already been defeated. The Soviet Union was not yet involved. The United Kingdom needed a powerful leader. Churchill answered the call.

In 1939 and 1940, the United Kingdom was on the defensive. Germany's powerful army had conquered Europe, including British troops fighting there. It seemed

Churchill's toughness helped him lead the United Kingdom during World War II.

MAN OF THE PEOPLE

Churchill was considered a man of the people. His speeches in support of the war effort were legendary. So too was his appearance in public. He was a military man and wartime leader. But he rarely set himself apart with a uniform. Churchill often dressed casually to meet the British people.

4

Number of volumes in Churchill's memoir of World War II.

- Churchill's personal determination helped the United Kingdom stand against Germany.
- He believed the United Kingdom could win against Germany.
- He enlisted the help of the United States and the Soviet Union.

nothing could stop Germany. An invasion of the United Kingdom was Germany's next step.

Churchill's first action as prime minister was unifying the British people. He gave speeches encouraging them to remain brave. He shared his unshakable desire to survive with the British people. He even banned talking about possible defeat. The United Kingdom had fewer troops and supplies than Germany had. Despite this, Churchill put his country on the attack. In September 1940, the United Kingdom won the Battle of Britain. Germany continued to bomb the United Kingdom by air. But it

would never try to invade the United Kingdom again during the war.

Churchill used his bravery and determination to gain support. He convinced the United States to supply the United Kingdom with tanks, planes, and bullets. He met with US President Franklin D. Roosevelt and Soviet Premier Joseph Stalin. With them, Churchill defeated Germany in World War II. But it was Churchill who traveled the most to maintain the relationship. Over the course of the war, he traveled 40,000 miles (64,374 km).

SHIRIN EBADI PROVIDES A VOICE FOR WOMEN

Shirin Ebadi is an Iranian lawyer. She fights for women's and children's rights. Despite many challenges, she has accomplished a lot in her career. Many of her feats had been considered unthinkable for a woman in Iran.

Ebadi was selected as a city court judge in Tehran in 1969. She was the first female judge in Iran. Five years later, she became the president of the Tehran city court. In 1979, she met her first big challenge. Iran's Islamic Revolution dramatically changed life in her nation. The democratic government disappeared. Instead, a Muslim cleric named Ayatollah Khomeini ran Iran. Women were viewed as inferior to men. Ebadi was removed as a judge. Women were not thought capable of serving the role.

By 1992, Ebadi had started her own law office. She took cases that challenged the government's authority. She fought for the right to speak up against the government. But her focus has been on the rights

Ebadi fights for human rights in Iran.

Ebadi's work has helped other Iranians stand up for human rights.

of women and children. Women still have few rights in Iranian society.

Ebadi founded two rights organizations in Iran. They both support Iranians in court. In 2003, she received a Nobel Peace Prize for her work. She was the first female Muslim and first Iranian to win the award.

3

Number of weeks Ebadi spent in jail in 2000 during one of her human rights cases.

- Ebadi is the first Muslim woman to win a Nobel Peace Prize.
- She fights for children's rights in Iran and around the globe.
- She is a pioneer of women's rights in Iran.

DEFENDER OF WOMEN AND CHILDREN

In one case, Ebadi fought to change custody laws in Iran. A young Iranian girl died in the care of her father and stepmother. The girl could not live with her mother. Iranian laws gave fathers favor over mothers. Ebadi was the mother's lawyer. She helped change the law to give mothers a better chance of getting custody.

QUEEN ELIZABETH I INSPIRES A KINGDOM

Queen Elizabeth I ruled England from 1588 to 1603. She showed the world women could lead nations. She was the daughter of King Henry VIII. She became queen in 1558 after the deaths of her siblings. At the time, people preferred men as leaders.

But Elizabeth I refused to give up her right to rule.

Elizabeth I was unlike any other leader. She never married. Some historians think she did not want a king to overtake her power. She was an intelligent woman who spoke six languages. She saw herself as a capable leader for her empire.

> Elizabeth I proved a queen could lead a nation.

COMMANDER ELIZABETH

Elizabeth I was also a capable military leader. She once visited the battlefield at Tilbury on the River Thames. British forces were preparing to fight the invading Spanish. The Spanish wanted a Catholic ruler in England. Elizabeth I inspired her troops with a rousing speech. Her troops went on to defeat the Spanish.

The English people supported Queen Elizabeth I during her reign.

Elizabeth's leadership helped unite England. At the time, Protestants and Catholics battled to control the government. Elizabeth I was a Protestant. Her rule gave control of the country to Protestants. But she did not mistreat Catholics. Instead, she allowed some Catholic traditions to continue.

With the country united, Elizabeth I created a Golden Age for England. Overseas trade for the empire expanded greatly. Arts and culture flourished at this time, too. Artists and writers created great works for Elizabeth I.

44

Number of years Elizabeth I was Queen of England.

- Elizabeth I refused to marry and allow a king to rule England.
- She unified her people and united English Protestants and Catholics.
- During her reign, trade and the arts flourished.

MAHATMA GANDHI FIGHTS GOVERNMENT ABUSES

Mahatma Gandhi was born in 1869. At the time, India was a British colony. Gandhi was a small, quiet man. But he had a big vision for India. After a long fight, his work helped India gain independence.

Gandhi believed fighting British rule without violence would embarrass the British. Gandhi had his first achievement in the 1920s. Poverty and hunger were big problems in his hometown. He led efforts to build new schools and hospitals. Gandhi wanted equal rights and services for Indians. But British rulers arrested him for causing trouble.

In the 1930s, Gandhi inspired Indians to buy only goods made in India. He wanted Indians to rely on themselves for goods, not on the British. In 1930, he led a march from his home to the coast. Supporters followed him more than 240 miles (386 km). They were protesting the British government. The British did not let Indian companies make and sell salt. Indians had to pay

Gandhi worked to improve the lives of Indians and gain independence for India.

a high tax on the salt they bought. Gandhi believed this treatment was not fair. The British government arrested Gandhi and tens of thousands of his supporters.

But the world noticed Gandhi's efforts. It also saw the poor treatment of Indians by the British. Gandhi believed the United Kingdom would be forced to grant India freedom. With the help of Gandhi's efforts, India gained independence in 1947.

Gandhi leads protesters on the march to the coast in 1930.

60,000
Estimated number of people arrested during Gandhi's march to the coast.

- Gandhi worked to gain India its freedom from British rule.
- He led a march protesting wrongdoing at the hands of the British.
- He influenced civil rights leaders in the United States.

WORLDWIDE IMPACT

Gandhi's beliefs inspired American civil rights leaders. African Americans such as Martin Luther King Jr. wrote to Gandhi. He helped them develop a plan for protesting without violence. These protests helped end segregation in America.

MARTIN LUTHER KING JR. WORKS FOR CIVIL RIGHTS

Slavery had ended after the Civil War (1861–1865). But in the 1950s, African Americans were still being treated unequally. Though slavery had ended, racism continued. Dr. Martin Luther King Jr. led the movement to gain equal rights for African Americans.

In the mid-twentieth century, southern African Americans lived in a segregated society. They used separate facilities from whites. Black children were taught in different schools. They faced racism at work. But King worked hard to change all this.

His first effort was leading the Montgomery bus boycott in 1955. African Americans were forced to give up their seats to white people. Often, they had to sit or stand at the back of the bus. In protest, many refused to use the city's buses. This cost the bus system of Montgomery, Alabama, a lot of money. It forced the system to end its policy of

King attends a press conference regarding segregation on buses and in restaurants.

381

Number of days the Montgomery bus boycott lasted.

- King fought for an end to segregation in the South.
- He taught people to protest without using violence.
- He worked for full voting rights for black voters.

THE VOTING RIGHTS ACT OF 1965

King also pushed for passage of the Voting Rights Act of 1965. The law made it easier for African Americans to vote. Without a vote, African Americans had no voice in government. Before, some towns and states required black voters to pass a test. Others made black voters pay a tax. The Voting Rights Act banned the use of these practices.

segregated busing. King and his supporters had won their first battle.

After this success, King arranged other protests. These protests called attention to inequality without using violence. But authorities in the South often responded with violence. King and his protestors were attacked with police dogs and water hoses. But he encouraged African Americans never to respond with violence. By 1964, the country finally acted. Congress passed the Civil Rights Act. The law made it illegal to deny work and services because of someone's race.

King worked to make it easier for African Americans to vote.

19

ABRAHAM LINCOLN PRESERVES THE UNION

Abraham Lincoln was elected president of the United States in 1860. The nation was in trouble. Southern leaders refused to end slavery. Northern states did not allow slavery. Many northerners wanted to end the practice across the country. Lincoln was one of these people.

President Lincoln immediately faced the threat of war. Slavery had existed since the nation's founding. It was a key issue in the election. Southern states left the Union to establish the Confederacy. Lincoln had to find a way to preserve the Union without destroying the South. He successfully led the Union army against the Confederacy in the Civil War (1861–1865).

But Lincoln's accomplishments were not limited to the war. He issued the Emancipation Proclamation in 1863. It freed all African-American slaves in the southern United States. Lincoln hoped to provide freedom to all Americans.

During his presidency, Lincoln also helped the country grow in size. The

During his presidency, Lincoln guided the Union and freed slaves in the South.

Homestead Act enabled people in the East to move out West. It gave them 160 acres (65 ha) of land if they built a home. The Morrill Act established public universities in every state. Lincoln preserved the Union and freed the slaves. He laid the foundation for future US expansion. His leadership changed the course of US history.

Lincoln speaks to Union officers on the battlefield at Antietam, Maryland, in 1862.

THINK ABOUT IT

Lincoln did many great things. But some of his acts were less honorable. He expanded the power the president had over Congress and the courts. He did this in the name of winning the war. Should the president be able to ignore laws when waging war? Why or why not?

11
Number of states where slaves were freed by the Emancipation Proclamation.

- Lincoln preserved the Union with smart leadership during the Civil War.
- He ended slavery in the southern United States.
- He supported laws that helped the United States expand westward.

21

NELSON MANDELA STOPS APARTHEID

White minority leaders controlled South Africa for decades. Members of the black majority lived in poverty in their own nation. Nelson Mandela brought equality and democracy to people suffering under apartheid.

Apartheid was a system of racial segregation in South Africa. There were more black people living in South Africa than white people. However, black people were forced to live separately from white people. They performed separate jobs. They attended separate schools.

Mandela was a leading voice in the campaign against apartheid. But his work put him in jail. He served a 27-year sentence. When he was finally released in 1990, he got back to work. He teamed up with President Frederik Willem de Klerk. They both knew the nation could not continue apartheid. Together, they helped establish basic freedoms and political rights for all South Africans.

In 1994, Mandela was elected president of South Africa. He was the first black leader of the nation. He led the country on a path toward healing. But he was more than a

Mandela fought for equal rights for black South Africans.

46664

46664 is a concert series named after Mandela's prison number. The concerts raise money to support HIV/AIDS research in Africa. HIV/AIDS is one of the greatest public health risks in Africa. In 2013, 35 million people in Africa were living with the disease. That same year, 1.5 million died as a result of it. Concerts are performed all over the world.

political leader. Mandela gave back in many ways. Foundations such as the Nelson Mandela Children's Fund change how society treats young children. They provide young African children with a voice.

27

Number of years Mandela spent in a prison for trying to end apartheid.

- Mandela fought for equal justice and freedoms in South Africa.
- He worked with the president of South Africa to end apartheid.
- He was the nation's first black leader.

Mandela shares the stage with President F. W. de Klerk (left).

FRANKLIN D. ROOSEVELT LEADS A NATION

Franklin D. Roosevelt was a US president. He was first elected in 1932. At the time, the country was in trouble. Many Americans were unemployed. Those who had jobs were making less money than they used to. The United States was struggling.

Roosevelt developed new policies called the New Deal. His programs gave the government new roles and power. He also made the government pay for many new services. Social Security was one of his creations. The program still provides financial support to elderly and disabled Americans.

Roosevelt was still president in 1939. That year, World War II (1939–1945) began in Europe.

But the American people wanted to stay out of the war. Roosevelt listened and kept the United States out of the war.

However, he did not ignore Europe. Instead, Roosevelt used US industry to support Britain and its allies

Roosevelt led the United States through financial turmoil and World War II.

against Germany. US tanks, planes, guns, and bullets were shipped to Europe. But this policy changed on December 7, 1941. Japan attacked a US navy base at Pearl Harbor in Hawaii. The event turned public opinion in favor of war. With the country behind Roosevelt, the United States entered the war.

Roosevelt changed the relationship presidents had with the public. He used radio, a new technology, to talk directly to the people. His radio addresses helped build a relationship between the president and the people.

The Civilian Conservation Corps was a New Deal program that put young men to work on public projects.

THINK ABOUT IT

Roosevelt is the only US president to serve four terms. He ignored the voluntary two-term limit all other presidents followed. He believed the president should not change when the country was in trouble. Many questioned his decision. Do you think it was wrong to continue leading? Why or why not?

15 million
Number of Americans out of work when Roosevelt took office.

- Roosevelt led the United States during World War II.
- He created new policies to lift America out of financial trouble.
- His new policies gave the government new rules and powers.

GEORGE WASHINGTON CHAMPIONS DEMOCRACY

George Washington shaped America and changed the world. He led the Continental Army during the American Revolution (1775–1783). The 13 American colonies fought for independence from England.

Washington's decisions and determination kept American soldiers on the field of battle. He convinced other leaders to support the cause.

But Washington was more than a war hero. The war ended in 1783. Washington wanted to return to a normal life. But the American people turned to him to lead the new country. First, he led the group of people who created the US Constitution. The document established the US government. He was offered the chance to be a king in America. But he believed people should elect their leaders.

Washington did not want to replace an English king with an American king. He did not want to lead the United States. But his fellow citizens elected him as the first US president.

George Washington helped win the Revolutionary War and shape the young United States.

A painting of Washington leading troops at Valley Forge, Pennsylvania

Washington served two four-year terms. He decided not to run again in 1796. Most future presidents followed his example.

Washington helped create a nation where citizens chose their leaders.

His influence is still seen today. For example, he supported the creation of national taxes and a national bank. Washington helped build the United States that exists today.

WASHINGTON THE SLAVEHOLDER

Washington was not a perfect man. Like many fellow white Americans at the time, he owned slaves. He never freed the 300 slaves he owned while he was alive. However, he did free them after his death. His will stated that his slaves would all be free after his wife's death.

8
Number of years Washington led the Continental Army.

- He was the first democratic president.
- He shaped the behavior and actions of future presidents.
- He believed in freedom of the people and leadership by men.

27

HOW YOU CAN MAKE CHANGE

Protest Peacefully

Many political leaders achieved success without using violence. Look around your neighborhood or school. If you find something that needs improving, take action. Write a polite letter to your mayor or principal. Ask friends and family members to sign the letter.

Sign a Petition

Petitions are written requests for change. To show their support, many people may sign a single petition. Is there something you would like to change at school or in your neighborhood? If so, write a petition asking for your principal or local government to make the change. With the help of an adult, gather as many signatures as you can to show your idea is supported by the community.

Write Your Representative or Senator

Is there a state or national law you would like to change? Even though kids cannot vote, they can write to their representatives and senators in the state capitol or Washington, DC. Write a polite letter stating your opinion. Be sure to include lots of reasons why you believe what you do.

GLOSSARY

boycott
Refuse to buy, use, or participate in activities as a way of protesting.

cavalry
Soldiers who fight on horseback.

cleric
A leader of a religion.

democratic
Based on a form of government in which people vote for leaders.

military
Relating to the armed forces, such as an army, navy, or air force.

politics
Activities relating to the policies and power of government.

poverty
The state of being poor.

prime minister
The head of the government in some countries.

protest
To say or do something that shows disagreement.

segregation
The practice of keeping people of different races separate.

FOR MORE INFORMATION

Books

McKenna, Amy, ed. *The 100 Most Influential World Leaders of All Time*. New York: Britannica Educational Publishing, 2010.

Murphy, Claire Rudolf. *Marching with Aunt Susan: Susan B. Anthony and the Fight for Women's Suffrage*. Atlanta: Peachtree, 2011.

Wilkinson, Philip. *Gandhi: The Young Protester Who Founded a Nation*. Washington, DC: National Geographic Society, 2005.

Websites

BBC: Queen Elizabeth I
www.bbc.co.uk/schools/primaryhistory/famouspeople/elizabeth_i

Kids.gov
www.kids.usa.gov

National Geographic Kids: Martin Luther King Jr.
www.kids.nationalgeographic.com/explore/history/martin-luther-king-jr

INDEX

About the Author

Matthew McCabe is a freelance writer and copywriter. He lives in Plymouth, Minnesota, raising his daughter and dog when he is not writing. He has worked as a writer for six years, covering a variety of topics ranging from business and travel to political leaders.